Words of Encouragement

J. Allen Loving

Words of Encouragement

J. Allen Loving

Altamont Media Publishing gratefully acknowledges the opportunity to assist Allen Loving in realizing his vision of publishing this work for God's glory. Truly, God the Father and Jesus Christ, the Son, are glorified in this work, and will be glorified through your encouragement also! The editor has retained the author's personal convention concerning punctuation in these poems.

Words of Encouragement

ISBN: 979-8-9873028-5-9
Printed in the United States of America
First Print Edition: January, 2026

Published by Altamont Media Publishing, LLC
Cover Design: Finch Ward
Interior Design & Typesetting: Ronnie W. Barnes Jr.

Cover & Title Font: **Delicious Sans**
Interior Fonts: **FUTURA BOLD** / Bookman Old Style

CONTENTS

CONTENTS (ALPHABETICALLY SORTED)

INTRODUCTION

A little about myself: my name is James Allen Loving. I was born in Columbia, SC on March 31, 1964.

Satan tried many times to kill me, but God protected me. And I never knew why until the idea of this book came around.

Now, how this book came to be. I suffered a stroke on June 8, 2020. This was the time when Covid was really bad, and no one could come to visit me in the hospital. After I came home my mom and dad came to spend time with me at home. During the time they were here, my mother suggested that I write a book of poems.

Through these poems, I hope that people can be encouraged in their walk with God.

My pastor, Ronnie Barnes, had published a book and was instrumental in helping me get this book published. So, a Big Thank You to him.

And to my wife Cathy, who has been with me now for 27 years, who has helped me and been by my side through all the ups and now the downs. She has been instrumental in transcribing my crudely written poems onto the computer. Without her, none of this would be possible. I love you, Cathy.

HOW TO READ THIS BOOK

Each poem in this collection was written to encourage your walk with God.

You may read one poem each day for reflection, or simply turn to any page when you need some spiritual encouragement.

Thank you for taking the time to read Words of Encouragement. May these words remind you that God is always near.

Notes:

Time With God Each Day

#1 - Written 12/31/2022

Make time to spend with God.

Each and every day.

A good way to start is when you wake up.

The first thing you do is pray,

“God use me to do your will.

Each person I meet your peace I pray they feel.

Whatever I say, whatever I do,

I pray somehow to glorify you”.

Notes:

Get Back to God

#2 - Written 12/31/2022

"God bless America" is what we used to say.

Now we see evil each and every day.

It's time to get back to God up above.

The one who died to show us His love.

Our leaders need God and we do too.

Until we get back to Him, what will we do?

Man makes promises they do not keep.

God loves us all, is what we need to teach.

Notes:

New Year's List

#3 - Written 1/03/2023

New Years is here.

Time for people to say what they want to do.

Then two or three weeks in not follow through.

Stop making goals you can't do.

Trust God to see you through.

Make time for God every day.

You will have a better life is what I say.

Notes:

Faith to Believe

#4 - Written 1/05/2023

Faith is believing something so, when it's not so, in order for it to be so.

That is easy when things have come,

Not how far you have to go.

God is with you when times are good,

And also, when they are bad.

Remember how far you have come!

There's no reason to be sad.

God will clear the way.

Then come back and walk with you.

Remember every day he never will leave you.

Satan wants you to doubt and think you are alone.

Just remember the path you are on.

To make Heaven your home.

Notes:

Loving Life Every Day

#5 - Written 1/26/2023

Loving Life each and every day.

Enjoy time you are given is what I have to say.

Spending time with God,

Will help you get through.

Satan tries to discourage,

Remember God is there for you,

Keep looking up, God will carry you.

As long as you let Him,

He'll always see you through.

So, keep the Faith,

Loving life daily.

Letting God lead you,

Completely not maybe.

Notes:

Easter: The Most Wonderful Time of the Year

#6 - Written 3/03/2023

It's the most wonderful time of the year.

Jesus died on the Cross, then rose from the grave.

He did all of this so we could be saved.

We need to be thankful every day.

Not just Easter.

But it is the most wonderful time of the year.

Remember follow Jesus every day.

He will never lead you astray.

Open your heart Jesus will come in.

Following Him you will always win.

Now let me be clear.

This truly is the most wonderful time of the year.

Notes:

When Springtime Comes

#7 - Written 4/03/2023

When springtime comes,

Flowers start to bloom.

Walking with Jesus,

You will never have gloom.

You may face some storms,

But sunny days are on the way.

Just keep faith in Jesus,

Cause He always finds a way.

Follow Him closely you can never go wrong.

It won't be long you'll sing a happy song.

Notes:

He’s Coming Back

#8 - Written 7/21/2023

You look around at what’s going on,

Nothing is right, everything is wrong.

Just remember Jesus said He’s coming back.

So, keep on praying looking toward the Eastern sky.

Jesus’ promises are true he cannot lie.

Keep the Faith every day.

Let others see you believing.

No matter what others may say.

Read the Bible continue to learn.

One day every knee will bow,

And every tongue confess He is Lord.

It doesn’t matter if it seems Satan is having his way.

The Bible tells us that it will come to an End.

So, keep looking up and Praying my Friend.

Notes:

The Perfect Place

#9 - Written 2/23/2024

Street of gold

Crystal sea

Sounds like the perfect place,

For you and me.

Jesus said he's coming back,

So, you know it's true.

That's good news for me and you.

No parting no pain

All is perfect all is great,

Seeing Jesus

Every day and night.

Notes:

Jesus Is There

#10 - Written 2/24/2024

When you are at the end of your rope,

Jesus is there.

When you think there is no hope,

Jesus is there.

When you are feeling low,

When you are in despair,

Jesus has you.

Don't give up hope,

Jesus is with you.

Just keep going — you'll make it through.

Never forget,

Jesus has got you.

Always remember,

Jesus is there.

Notes:

Look Up Toward Heaven

#11 - Written 3/16/2024

When you are feeling down,

Look up toward heaven.

When you feel like you cannot go,

Cry out to Jesus.

When you are climbing up that mountain,

Remember He is with you.

Things will get better,

So, keep on going.

It will get better.

So, keep on moving.

God has got you.

Keep that in mind.

Before you know it,

Bad things will be behind.

Notes:

Wisdom in Proverbs

#12 - Written 3/23/2024

The Book of Proverbs Chapter 1, verses 1-12,

Contains wisdom if you will read.

Not just read but take time to study.

Read slow so it will sink in.

The words you read,

Will let you know,

That Jesus is your best friend.

They will guide you the right way.

If you follow them,

And do not stray.

Study the words in Proverbs.

As you read it,

And have devotions each and every day.

It contains 31 chapters,

Use it as a devotional,

Then you can pray.

Notes:

Turn to God

#13 - Written 3/23/2024

When things are looking bad don't,

Turn from God turn to Him.

Don't listen to Satan.

Things will get better.

Just keep on praying.

You will get your answer.

Be just like Job.

Things will get better.

So, keep your eyes on God.

The answer will come,

Yes, no or later.

He will answer your prayers.

Just turn to God.

Because he has got you.

There is nothing in the world He cannot do.

Notes:

The Question

#14 - Written 3/28/2024

The most important question there is,

Is if you died today,

Do you know you will go to heaven?

If your answer is, “I think so”

Or “I’m not sure”

Then the answer is no.

You need to make sure of where you will go.

The Bible says we all have sinned and

Fallen short of the glory of God.

That means we all have to pray.

So, if you want to make sure say these words,

“Jesus, I believe you are the son of God,

And I believe you died for me.

I know I am a sinner so; I ask you today.

To forgive me and wash my sins away”.

Notes:

Easter Everyday

#15 - Written 3/30/2024

It's Easter when we celebrate,

The day Jesus rose from the grave.

But we need to remember this every day.

If He's in your heart you need to rejoice,

Let others see you are happy.

And hear it in your voice.

From the time you rise,

Til you go to sleep,

Don't let it be a surprise,

If Jesus is of who you seek.

So, celebrate Easter every day.

If in your heart is where

Jesus does stay.

Notes:

Do What You Can

#16 - Written 9/11/2024

Do what you can,

Jesus will do the rest.

He will be with you,

No matter the test.

How high the mountain,

Or wide the sea.

He will be with you,

Hand in hand He will be.

Notes:

Keep The Faith

#17 - Written 9/11/2024

Why is it when something bad happens,

People say,

Why would God do this to me?

But when things are good,

They don't say thank you God.

In good times or bad,

Keep the faith.

Because God is with you,

All of the time.

Thank Him and Praise Him.

Because what is bad will be good.

God is always with you,

Day and night.

Keep the faith,

Everything will be alright.

Notes:

God Has You in His Hand

#18 - Written 10/19/2024

Things may look bad,

But don't be sad.

God has you in His hand.

Things may be gone,

God understands.

He will not leave you alone.

Things lost are of this world.

And like Job,

God will restore.

What you lost and even more.

Remember God has you,

That is true.

So, keep looking up,

And don't give up.

Written after hurricane Helene 2024

Notes:

God is Always There

#19 - Written 11/02/2024

When surrounded by darkness

Look for the Light.

God is always there

With you in His sight.

Keep the Faith.

When Satan comes

Whatever the cost

Jesus defeated him

At the cross.

Keep on moving, never give in

God has seen you through

Again, and again.

This is just another valley.

You have to go through.

But do not worry

God is there with you.

Notes:

Keep On Climbing

#20 - Written 11/13/2024

When climbing the mountains,

You may fall.

It's not how many times you fall,

But how many you get up.

Keep the faith.

Never give up.

When you reach the top,

It is easier going down.

The battle is won.

And victory is on the other side.

Give God the glory,

For what he has done.

He is with you all the time,

Through the good and the bad.

So, keep on going and never be sad.

Notes:

No Need to Run

#21 - Written 12/25/2024

When you are walking on the path and

You feel like Satan is chasing you,

Don't run just keep on walking,

God has got you.

He has beat the devil so many times,

Satan should know he can't win.

God has you to beat him again.

So, don't give up, He's still got you.

Just like all the other times.

Notes:

The Greatest Gift

#22 - Written 12/25/2024

It's December 2024 and Christmas

Draws near once more.

Do we remember or forget the

Greatest gift ever given?

When we are told about God's Son

Coming from Heaven.

When the Bible tells us that God gave

His only Son so we can be saved and

Spend eternity in Heaven or

Is our focus on trees and how many

Gifts will we get instead,

Or remember the greatest gift.

As we count all the packages under

The tree and count with greatness and wonder

How many of these are for me?

It's time to focus back on God's only

Son and let us remember.

The greatest gift that should be number one.

Notes:

Between Two Thieves

#23 - Written 1/01/2025

Jesus died on a cross,

Between two thieves.

It is strange how someone,

So Holy could die between them.

He came to this world for all of us to save.

Died such a cruel death,

To rise from the grave.

We all need to seek Him and

Find Him each day.

Do our best to follow Him along life's way.

He should be the light that lights our path,

Each and every day.

The one we try to follow as we travel life's way.

Notes:

Resurrection

#24 - Written 1/03/2025

Jesus said Lazarus, come forth.

So, all the dead would not rise.

Because if they did, they would fill the sky.

And it was not time for the Resurrection to take place.

And Satan see the end of Death in his face.

But that day is coming, that every knee shall bow

And tongue confess

And even the sinners see Jesus is the Best.

Notes:

Forgive Them

#25 - Written 1/06/2025

When Jesus was on the cross,

He said forgive them Father,

They know not what they do.

This was to forgive the sinners,

And the future ones too.

Then He said it is finished.

To show He has finished all He came to do.

Except, be placed in the tomb then come forth too.

Notes:

Jesus Knows All

#26 - Written 1/22/2025

The doctor walks in and says no.

Then Jesus follows and says I don't think so.

Man, only knows what he has learned,

But Jesus knows all.

From beginning to end.

He knows what the future holds for you.

So, if He says no, it will become true.

You can listen to man or follow Jesus to the End.

The choice made is up to you.

Follow Jesus or follow man.

Jesus knows all, but man knows what he can.

Notes:

Walking With Jesus

#27 - Written 1/27/2025

Walking with Jesus every day,

Where He leads, I will follow.

Reading my Bible every day,

Learning what Jesus taught.

Praying to get closer and fellowship because,

You never know when you see someone

That needs a smile

Or word of encouragement.

Notes:

All For Me

#28 - Written 2/08/2025

Jesus took the stripes for our healing,

Died on the cross for our saving.

Rose from the grave for our living.

Went to Heaven for our eternity.

Coming back for us to be together forever.

Notes:

Faith

#29 - Written 5/11/2025

All Christians have faith,

Some large,

Some small.

It doesn't matter how much,

You can always get more.

Just spend time with God.

And He will strengthen you.

You will be amazed,

At all He can do.

You will believe more, as your faith grows.

And get closer to God, as your faith grows.

You will see things happen that you have been praying for.

And give God the Glory,

That you were thinking would never take place.

And people will see a new Glory on your face.

Notes:

Heaven

#30 - Written 5/23/2025

One day the sky will open, and Jesus will come back.

All of the Christians will go to heaven.

The sinners will be left behind.

What a great day it will be.

And all of the things we will see what we have read and heard about will be around.

No more sickness, no more pain, no death ever again.

The crystal sea and street of Gold,

All the wonders to behold.

Notes:

Heaven or Hell: You Choose

#31 - Written 5/25/2025

Christians go to heaven; sinners go to hell.

All is great for Christians,

Sinners think all will be well.

For Christians all is perfect,

Sinners say, “I will have friends there.”

Christians will Rejoice,

Sinners live in torment for all Eternity.

Heaven sounds great,

It’s the place for me.

Make your choice before it’s too late.

Jesus died for all,

So, you can choose your fate.

It is for Eternity, where you want to be?

Notes:

Raise Children Right

#32 - Written 5/26/2025

Parents do their best to raise children right.

But you don't know what happens when they are out of sight.

They are around kids that don't come from a happy home.

So, they want everyone sad and will not leave happy kids alone.

They tell them lies each and every day until the good kids finally run away.

They lie on their family and no longer see.

So, the parents pray for the child and hope in Heaven together they will be.

God sees again for what has gone wrong.

So, keep on believing because the family behold is strong.

Notes:

Take That First Step

#33 - Written 5/27/2025

You don't know how far you can go,

Until you take that first step.

You may be called to preach but you will not know unless you try.

So, open your Bible and start to read.

See what God reveals to you.

Teaching may be your call see how you feel.

Singing may be your thing so, open your mouth, and give it a try.

You never know until you try, until you take that first step.

God will be with you all along the way,

Guiding you each and every day.

Notes:

Keep Your Trust in God

#34 - Written 5/28/2025

People come and go.

But God is always there.

People leave when times get tough,

But God doesn't care.

God will hold you by your hand,

And always see you through.

As long as you depend on God,

There's nothing He can't do.

So, don't put your trust in man,

But always talk to God.

God will send Angels to help when it seems like there is no one else.

So, never give up, but keep looking up.

And above all else, remember you are never by yourself.

Notes:

My First Day in Heaven

#35 - Written 6/01/2025

How great that first day in Heaven will be.

To see the Gates of pearl and street of Gold.

Sitting by the crystal sea, no more suffering, no more pain.

Everything will be perfect again.

Seeing all the saints that have gone on before.

No more saying goodbye anymore, to spend time with Jesus,

Each and every day.

The one that made it possible when He died for me that day.

Singing songs old and new, seeing saints that you never knew.

What a great day they all will be,

But how special that first day and all you will see.

People missing that you thought would be there that you thought were saved but you do not see.

Oh, how great that first day will be.

Notes:

God Is Always with You

#36 - Written 6/03/2025

I can do all things through Christ, because He is always with me.

He died on a cross to save my soul.

Now eternal life is what I have.

Because Jesus is not in a tomb or in a grave.

Giving His life for all to save.

He took the stripes for me to be healed.

So, no matter how bad things seem,

God can do anything but fail.

So, keep moving on, because He is with you.

Notes:

Jesus Loves Me

#37 - Written 6/05/2025

Jesus loves me this I know,

Because I read my Bible every day.

When things start to get tough, I go to Him and pray.

He's there to help me all along life's way.

I make time for Him each and every day.

I don't just talk to Him when time runs out.

I make time to talk to Him and tell Him when I have doubt.

He answers my prayers all on His time.

I remind myself He has not left me behind.

For Jesus loves me this I know.

Notes:

You Will Win

#38 - Written 6/13/2025

Read your Bible every day and make time to pray.

Going down the mountain is easier than going up.

But remember God is with you every step of the way.

He has you by the hand and will never let you go.

Satan will tempt you as you read in the Bible.

He even did this to Jesus when He took the form of man.

But scripture will beat him every time and he will run away.

He cannot stand the word of God and it will be you and God again traveling along hand in hand.

So, keep moving on and never lose your Faith.

God is with you, and you will win.

Notes:

Jesus Walks In

#39 - Written 6/21/2025

When things are looking bad, and your Faith is getting thin.

When it looks like there is no way that you can win.

That is when Jesus walks in.

He will make everything right.

So, keep your eyes on the light.

It may look like things are getting dim, at that moment Jesus walks in.

No matter what you are going through, He will do it again and again.

So, keep the Faith and never give in.

Because Jesus will walk in again and again.

Just keep the door open so Jesus can walk in again.

Notes:

Heaven for Eternity

#40 - Written 6/22/2025

One day my soul's gonna fly through the sky.

And it will not be an airplane ride.

I am heading to Heaven to spend eternity.

Don't you wanna come with me gone from this world.

No more worries no more fears everything that made it bad here.

Read the Bible you will see the way that Jesus made a way.

Open your eyes so you can see.

You will live in Heaven for eternity.

Notes:

A FINAL WORD

Allen and Cathy here! We wanted to say thank you again for reading this book.

If you are looking for a church to attend, we go to Laurens Pentecostal Holiness Church on 26 Wallace St. in Laurens, SC.

If you have any questions about this book or just want to say hello you can contact me at cathyloving01@gmail.com.

If you need more copies, you can go to Amazon.com to order them. That directly supports us.

Go from dream to done with
Altamont Media Publishing.

www.AltamontMedia.net

inquire@altamontmedia.net

www.ingramcontent.com/pod-product-compliance
Lightning Source LLC
LaVergne TN
LVHW020653100826
845148LV00012B/2459

* 9 7 9 8 9 8 7 3 0 2 8 5 9 *